Towards Effective Teaching

Learning From Jesus

Edwin Pugh

Kingdom Publishers

Towards Effective Teaching
Copyright© Edwin

All rights reserved. No part of this book may be reproduced in any form by photocopying or any electronic or mechanical means, including information storage or retrieval systems, without permission in writing from both the copyright owner and the publisher of the book. The right of Edwin to be identified as the author of this work has been asserted by him in accordance with the Copyright, Designs and Patents Act 1988 and any subsequent amendments thereto.
A catalogue record for this book is available from the British Library.
All Scripture Quotations have been taken from the New International Version.

ISBN: 978-1-913247-51-5

1st Edition by Kingdom Publishers
Kingdom Publishers
London, UK.

You can purchase copies of this book from any leading bookstore or email **contact@kingdompublishers.co.uk**

"Come follow me" Jesus said, *"and I will make you fishers of men."*

Matthew 4:19

Contents

Introduction	9
Section 1: Teaching a Group	**11**
Establishing a good teaching environment	14
Cultivating Motivated learners	16
Captivating your audience	18
Personalising your message	20
Building on prior knowledge	22
Speaking with authority	24
Using illustrations	27
Keeping the listeners' attention	29
Providing guidelines	31
Summarising your teaching	33
Evaluating your teaching	35
Checklist	37
Section 2: Giving a Demonstration	**39**
Having a clear aim	43
Being seen and heard	44
Being clear in your instructions	45
Involving the learner	46
Encouraging audience participation	47
Making sure the key audience see	48
Evaluating the impact of the demonstration	49
Finishing with a word of encouragement	51
Checklist	52

Section 3: Using a Case Study   53
Choosing a familiar case   57
Involving the learners at the time   59
Guiding the learners to apply the case study   60
Checklist   61

Section 4: Using an Allegory or Parable   63
Keeping the stories short   67
Building on previous understanding   69
Making the story believable   71
Making the story personal   72
Ending with a challenge   73
Checklist   74

Section 5: Being a Mentor   75
Asking probing questions   78
Helping resolve arguments   79
Comforting through difficult times   80
Praying for your student   82
Checklist   83

Section 6: Setting a Practical Project   85
Giving an induction   88
Giving instructions   89
Carrying out a debriefing   90
Checklist   91

Section 7: Qualities of a Christian Teacher   93
Requirements of Christian Teachers   97
Checklist   99
Dedication   100

Introduction

> Therefore, go and make disciples of all nations, baptising them in the name of the Father and of the Son and of the Holy Spirit, and teaching them to obey everything I have commanded you.
>
> *Matthew 28: 19-20*

Jesus gave His disciples their Great Commission at the end of the Gospel of Matthew. It is a call to all Christians to help people become followers of Jesus and to live a Christian life modelled on Christian principles. To do this Christians are required to teach.

Teaching is not something that comes naturally to many people. It is an art to be learnt.

To deliver God's message and commandments most effectively it is imperative that we, as teachers, are equipped. Whether as church leader, or simply as a committed Christian we will all become more effective if we take time to learn and continue learning to be able to teach more effectively. What better way than to learn from Jesus whose teachings have transformed millions of lives and continue to transform our world.

Drawing on examples from the Gospels , this short book looks at some of the methods Jesus used in teaching his disciples his spiritual truths. It shows how he captivated the imaginations of those listening, how he instilled them with God's truths and equipped them to do His work. Examples are given of him preaching, mentoring, giving a demonstration and setting a project for his followers.

Teaching is not just about technique. It is about who you are. Drawing on Jesus we look at the qualities required to be an effective Christian teacher.

This book is written for those who wish to become better teachers as well as those who are interested in catching a glimpse of the techniques Jesus used.

Section 1

Teaching a Group

Refer to the Gospel of Matthew Chapters 5, 6 and 7

Section 1: **Teaching a Group**

The Sermon on the Mount in Chapters 5, 6 and 7 of the Gospel of Matthew is one of the best known examples of Jesus teaching to a crowd. This text does not address whether the Sermon was delivered at one sitting or whether it is a compilation of teachings presented on numerous occasions. The lessons on teaching technique can be learnt irrespective of this opinion.

At the Sermon on the Mount Jesus is teaching a large group of people. Teaching groups is a situation regularly encountered by educationalists and church leaders. The challenge for teaching each group is the same. How can you make the message very clear? How do you maintain the interest of the listeners? How do you make it relevant to the listeners' lives? In terms of the Gospel, how do you make the message so compelling as to transform the listeners' lives? How do you direct it to each one of the audience so that it is seen and embraced as personal to each one?

Using the Sermon on the Mount we can draw out key lessons from Jesus to apply in our own teaching.

Establishing a Good Teaching Environment

> Now when he saw the crowds, he went up on a mountainside and sat down. His disciples came to him, and he began to teach them...
> Matthew 5:1-2

"Are you sitting comfortable children? Then I'll begin"....so began the daily story telling in the very old television programme for children called 'Watch with mother'. As a child I could not wait to hear the story that was to follow. I was sitting comfortably and ready and receptive to savour and digest the story that followed.

How many times have you sat through sermons or lectures where you could not hear or see properly? Where the room was too hot or too cold? How many times have you or others been distracted through unnecessary noise? The unwelcome ringing of mobile phones is a current example. How many times have you endured teaching in an environment where you were not comfortable? Giving thought to establishing the right environment can aid learning . This includes appropriate seating for the audience as well as the platform for the speaker. It includes making sure the listeners are not distracted.

Jesus did not end up on the mountain by chance. When he saw the crowds, *he went up* on a mountainside....Jesus planned where he would deliver his lecture. He looked around and decided on the best spot. It was the custom of the day for rabbi teachers to be seated when teaching. Jesus' audience would recognise he was about to teach. Choosing the sloping auditorium of the mountainside allowed Jesus to be seen and heard by all.

Teaching Tips

- Do all you can to make your listeners comfortable
- Make sure the listeners can see and hear you
- Try and preempt unnecessary distractions

The Good Teaching Environment Checklist

Are the seating arrangements the best they can be?

Can everyone see and hear?

Is the room temperature and lighting appropriate?

Are you, as teacher, able to make eye contact with every listener?

Have you removed distractions such as unnecessary noise? *For example ensuring mobile phones are switched off?*

Cultivating Motivated Learners

> His disciples *came to him*, and he began to teach them,.....
> Matthew 5:1b-2

Notice that the disciples 'came to him'. Jesus did not just stop where he was and start speaking. Not only did he pick the best place to teach but he required the learners to come to him. They had to follow him and do a little climbing. They had to show motivation. In one way it would be very unlikely for them to make the effort and then choose to ignore the teaching. They clearly wanted to hear what he had to say.

Have you ever not wanted to go and hear someone teach? What about the uninspiring preacher who speaks in a monotone in highly academic, apparently non-practical terms, seemingly unrelated to the present day? Remember the teacher or preacher who bored you to tears?

Adults are motivated to learn for a variety of reasons. Some common motives are:

- To learn or develop new ideas
- To follow up an interest
- To satisfy curiosity
- To obtain a qualification
- To hear a charismatic speaker

It is also recognised that an educator's style, commitment and enthusiasm are all major motivating factors in helping people to learn. People respond to teachers who show genuine concern and interest in them and who interact with them.

For adults there will be times when their motivation to learn is low. Some disincentives are:

- Lack of purpose
- An hostile atmosphere
- An uncomfortable environment
- An unfriendly speaker

The challenge for teachers is to create an expectation and ambience in which the learner wants to learn. Teachers need to be engaging and enthusiastic for their topic. They must be seen to practice what they preach. The environment needs to be conducive to learning. The topic needs to be attractive and relevant to the learner.

In Christian circles there is an enormous motivation for people to learn about the Gospels and Jesus. If the promise of Jesus that they can receive eternal life is not a motivation then nothing is!

Teaching Tip

- Try to ensure that the learners are motivated to learn

Captivating Your Audience

And he began to teach them, saying:
Blessed are the poor in spirit,
For theirs is the kingdom of heaven.
Blessed are those who mourn,
For they will be comforted.
Blessed are the meek,
For they will inherit the earth.
Blessed are those who hunger and thirst for righteousness,
For they will be filled.
Blessed are the merciful,
For they will be shown mercy.
Blessed are the pure in heart,
For they will see God.
Blessed are the peacemakers,
For they will be called sons of God.
Blessed are those who are persecuted
Because of their righteousness,
For theirs is the kingdom of heaven.

Blessed are <u>you</u>…..
Matthew 5: 3-11

It is important to engage your audience right at the beginning of any talk or sermon. This will make them want to listen and learn more.

Blessed had a distinct meaning for the listeners. It describes a state of true happiness. Not an emotional happiness dependent on outward circumstances but a state of inner fulfilment and spiritual joy. It was a state of spiritual contentedness. Who could not want to be blessed? What a motivation to listen, to sit up and take notice.

This discourse on 'Being blessed' was not a topic plucked randomly from the air. It was a subject specifically chosen by Jesus in response to the needs and desires of his audience. Jesus knew what his audience needed at that time to increase their spiritual understanding. He appeals directly to the self interest of every individual listening.

Blessed are..., blessed are..., blessed are...eight 'blesseds'. Eight hard hitting truths that at face value seem to be about some other people. Eight truths that leave the audience thinking who is he talking about? I want to learn more. I want to be blessed. The ninth reiteration of blessed brings the reality home to them. Blessed are you. The listener realises that this is about them. It comes as a surprise and is deeply personal to each one. They can be blessed. In a sense the fisherman had them hooked. My guess is that those listening were completely transfixed and couldn't wait to hear more.

There is an old teaching maxim that states that there are two key tactics for reinforcing learning. Firstly, if anything is worth saying, it is worth saying twice. Secondly, if anything is worth saying, it is worth saying twice. Jesus reinforces blessed nine times. It is very important and will be remembered by the listeners.

Teaching Tips

- Make sure the opening is designed to gain and hold the listener's attention.
- Reiterate important points.
- Have a personal application but don't always make it obvious at the start; bring an element of surprise.
- Appeal to the self-interest of your audience. *This implies knowing it!*

Personalising Your Message

> *You are* the salt of the earth. But if the salt looses its saltiness, how can it be made salty again? It is no longer good for anything, except to be thrown out and trampled by men.
> *You are* the light of the world. A city on a hill cannot be hidden. Neither do people light a lamp and put it under a bowl. Instead they put it on its stand, and it gives light to everyone in the house. In the same way let <u>your</u> light shine before men, that they may see <u>your</u> good deeds and praise <u>your</u> father in heaven
>
> *Matthew 5: 13, 14*

"You are..."

"Who me?"

"Yes you!"

Jesus did not say *"Some people* are the salt of the earth", He said *"You are"*

This message was not applicable to someone else. This teaching had a direct bearing on each and every listener. It was personally applicable and a challenge to each one. Of course it was not didactic in the sense they had no choice. Jesus gave them both sides of the argument. They were either salt or they were not. They would either let their light shine or it would be covered.

Jesus did not stop after telling his listeners the uplifting and comforting consequences of their choice. He continued by telling the negative. He told it as it was, not shirking the hard truth. In not being salt they could be "thrown out and trampled on". At the end of the message everyone knew the consequences of their choice. Which way did they want it? This message was deeply personal. It could not be deflected or transferred to someone else. Each one could choose to be this, or that. Jesus wanted them to follow him. My guess is they had to hear more.......

People are more likely to listen and learn if the topic being taught is directly relevant to them. Sitting through an academic treatise which has no apparent individual relevance or practical applicability will stimulate the unusual few rather than the majority. Teaching God's truths needs to hit at the individual heart and have the potential to influence the life of each person listening.

Teaching Tips

- Make the message applicable to each one present.
- Challenge each one.
- Explain any consequences, both positive and negative.
- Do not shirk from telling the truth.

Building on Prior Knowledge

You have heard that it was said to the people long ago,' Do not murder,...'
You have heard that it was said, 'Do not commit adultery.'
Again, *you have heard it said* to the people long ago,' Do not break your oath,...'
You have heard that it was said, 'Eye for an eye and tooth for a tooth.'
You have heard that it was said,' Love your neighbour and hate your enemy.'

Matthew 5: 21, 27,33,38,43

One of the challenges faced by teachers is knowing at what level to pitch their talk. Different learners may be at different stages of learning. Some individuals will know very little, if anything, about the Gospels. Others may be very mature in their faith with a broad knowledge. In adult education it is proven good practice to base the foundation of teaching on what the listeners already know. This makes it easier for learners to understand and take forward their learning. Jesus does this by basing his teaching on scriptures which will have been well known to his audience He establishes his educational base and builds upon it.

It is common sense to realise that you are unlikely to grasp trigonometry unless you have at least a grasp of basic maths. There is the maxim that you should not run before you can walk. Good teachers will take students through an understanding of basics to create a foundation on which to build to more advanced learning. The difficulty is that in an unselected audience there may be individuals at different stages of understanding. Their knowledge bases will differ. They will be of mixed ability.

A recognised educational tactic is to try to create a common knowledge base for the whole audience on which to advance the teaching and help the learners advance their knowledge and understanding. To do this the teacher illustrates or reiterates the basic knowledge on which they will build to take the learner to the next level of understanding.

Teaching Tips

- Recognise variation in your audience both in basic knowledge and ability.
- Establish a common level of knowledge or understanding
- Build from the established foundation

Speaking with Authority

> You have heard that it was said to the people long ago,' Do not murder...' But I tell you
> You have heard that it was said, 'Do not commit adultery.' But I tell you
> Again, you have heard it said to the people long ago,' Do not break your oath...' But I tell you
> You have heard that it was said, 'Eye for an eye and tooth for a tooth.' But I tell you
> You have heard that it was said,' Love your neighbour and hate your enemy.' But I tell you
>
> *Matthew 5: 21-22, 27-28, 33-34, 38-39, 43-44*

Good teachers will know their topic. They will have researched and become expert at their subject. They will have appropriate references to back up their statements and develop their argument. They speak with authority. Learners can see that the teacher knows her/his topic.

There is no doubting Jesus spoke with great authority. For each of the areas the audience had been reminded of, Jesus categorically gave them his considered opinion - "But I tell you". He moved their knowledge and understanding forward based on his undoubted mastery of the topic he was teaching.

For each of us as teachers, our instruction will not be confidently believed unless we are seen to know our topic. Having street credibility certainly helps status. In moving a learner's understanding from level A to level B it is imperative we are at least at level B. The level of knowledge within a group of people will vary enormously. There will be a range of the level of knowledge of individuals, from those who may not have heard of the Gospel, to those 'expert' theologians who know it in Greek and Hebrew and are able to argue each jot and tittle. As potential teachers we can try to identify those whose knowledge base and understanding is less than ours. We can then build on their level of knowledge and help improve it to at least the level of our own.

> Again, you have heard what it was said to the people long ago, 'Do not break your oath *(Leviticus 19:12),* but keep the oaths you have made to the Lord'. *(Numbers 30:20, Deuteronomy 23:21),* But I tell you, Do not swear at all: either by heaven, for it is God's throne*(Isaiah 66:1)*; or by the earth, for it is His footstool; or by Jerusalem, for it is the city of the Great King.*(Psalm 48:2).*
>
> Matthew 5:33-35

Jesus had a thorough detailed knowledge of the Old Testament scriptures, the scriptures used to teach the Jews of the time. The beatitudes are laced with references to the Old Testament. Jesus did not rely solely on his authority and charisma. His statements are reinforced by the evidence. His claims are developed on fact and prior undisputed teachings.

To enable good learning people need the facts. Anecdote by itself is not enough. Not only should the facts be presented but also the evidence that established the facts. This presumes there is always evidence. Each of us will have more confidence in being operated on by a surgeon who has studied his/her trade and is carrying out operations in line with what scientific evidence has proved to produce the best results, rather than the surgeon who is less orthodox and does not have that detailed knowledge.

In teaching we should strive to not only know our topic but also know the evidence behind it. In teaching biblical truths we should try not only to know the principles, but also the scriptures which underpin the principles. When challenged as teachers we can refer to the authoritative source of the evidence. For Christians it is imperative that we are familiar with the contents of the bible.

Teaching Tips

- Know your topic.
- Base any teaching on solid fact and references.
- Assemble a range of scriptural references to support your teaching.

Using Illustrations

The Concept

You have heard what it was said, 'Eye for an eye, and tooth for tooth.' But I tell you, do not resist an evil person.

Four practical examples

(i) If someone strikes you on the right cheek , turn to him the other also. (ii) And if someone wants to sue you and take your tunic, let him have your cloak as well. (iii) If someone forces you to go one mile, go with him two miles. (iv) Give to the one who asks you, and do not turn away from the one who wants to borrow from you.

Matthew 5:38 – 42

Giving illustrations as part of teaching can help individuals better grasp a concept. Giving a practical example can make teaching more real.

It can be argued that teaching is not worth much unless it produces a change in attitude or behaviour. Using an illustration from the health field, it is of no value to the health of the learner to simply acquire the knowledge that eating the 'wrong' foods leads to poor health, if it does not result in the learner changing their dietary habits. In the same way it is of no value to the spiritual well being of the listener to simply acquire head-knowledge of spiritual truths. True value comes in applying the truths and applying it to our lives appropriately.

The illustrations used by Jesus not only tell us the spiritual truth. They also clearly indicate how we are to behave in response to the truth. They are illustrations with which the listeners will be familiar. They apply to each one as Jesus has again personalised the message. 'If someone strikes you (!)....' yes you! The illustrations invite each listener to imagine the situation and apply it to their lives. The concept becomes real and applicable to their lives. It is relevant and more likely to be remembered when the teaching is over.

As teachers we should try to illustrate or clarify our teaching with examples we can recognise and apply in our everyday lives. This grounds the teaching in reality. It says to the listener, "This is what this means in *your* life".

Teaching Tips

- Give focussed practical real-life illustrations
- Make the illustrations personal and relevant
- Indicate the behaviour change expected

Keeping the Listeners' Attention

Some lectures can be notoriously boring. We have all been in a lecture or sermon with the teacher or preacher seeming to drone on interminably, speaking at us, not to us.

The picture of individuals dozing off during lectures in school and university is well recognised. Even the most attentive listener can start to mini-doze. It is well recognised that most listeners' attention span starts to stray after approximately 20 minutes. For some it may be shorter. Listeners need to be jolted from potential inattention or sleep. Jesus does this by intermittently firing personal questions to his audience which directly challenge each one. He is heard to ask each one his/ her opinion. Of course the questions were rhetorical in that Jesus was not expecting the audience to shout out the answer.

Jesus directs sixteen questions at the listeners in the Matthew's account of the beatitudes; sixteen questions in just over one hundred verses of Jesus teaching. Half of these questions are personalised and aimed directly at the listener…..

> On teaching 'Love your Enemies' *Matthew 5:43-48*
> If *you* love those who love you, what reward will *you* get? *(v 46)*
> ..if *you* greet only your brothers, what are *you* doing more than others? *(v47)*
>
> On teaching 'Do not Worry' *Matthew 6:25-34*
> Are *you* not more valuable than they? *(v26)*
> Who of *you* by worrying can add a single hour to his life? Matthew *(v27)*
> And why do *you* worry about your clothes? Matthew *(v28)*
>
> On teaching ' Do not Judge Others' *Matthew 7:1-6*
> Why do *you* look at the speck of sawdust in your brother's eye and pay no attention to the plank that is in your own? *(v3)*

> How can *you* say to your brother,' Let me take the speck out of your eye,' when all the time there is a plank in your own? *(v4)*
>
> On teaching 'Ask, Seek. Knock' *Matthew 7:7-12*
> Which of *you*, if his son asks for bread will give him a stone? *(v9)*
> Or if he asks for a fish *(which of you)* will give him a snake? *(v10)*

The questions make the listener reflect on their own reaction to the teaching scenario. What would they do? How would they react? Why do they behave as they do? They are challenging and stimulating – designed to keep the listeners alert and on their toes.

When teaching we can try to design questions which are challenging and apparently aimed at each individual in the audience. The questions should be such that their full answer can only be given if the learner has been alert and listened to the prior teaching. Having the questions regularly interspersed in the 'talk' will ensure that the learner stays attentive and listens.

Teaching Tip

- Ask rhetorical questions of the audience which are personal and challenging but not designed to embarrass individuals.

Providing Guidelines

I have a confession. My personality is such that I am too impatient to follow instructions. This manifested itself when I was a child building model aeroplanes. Invariably I could not get the pilot into the cockpit as the cockpit cover was already glued tight. I had jumped from step 45 to 50 and missed the steps in between. It now manifests itself when I buy flat-pack self assembly furniture. Invariably I have to unscrew some part and restart as I'd thought I knew what to do. Building both model airplanes and flat-pack furniture requires specific step by step instructions or guidelines.

Guidelines or practical instructions are useful for us to ensure we follow an appropriate course of action. They help make a complex matter more manageable. They give a logical order in doing things to ensure the end product is as it should be. They can be shared so others can do the same. They can be taught. Jesus teaches his listeners several sets of guidelines in the Beatitudes. The most well known is the Lord's Prayer.

This, then is how you should pray:

> Our Father in heaven,
> Hallowed be your name,
> Your kingdom come,
> Your will be done
> On earth as it is in heaven.
> Give us this day our daily bread.
> Forgive us our debts,
> As we also have forgiven our debtors.
> And lead us not into temptation, but deliver us from the evil one.

Matthew 6:9-13

A guideline for prayer is given which has been learnt by many, taught by many and which has been recognised as good practice through the 2000 years since it was given. A powerful teaching technique, don't you think?

> Guidelines are also given for fasting. *"But when you fast, put oil on your head and wash your face". (Matthew 6:17)*

Guidelines can be aids to learning. If teachers wish to give a set of instructions, guidelines could be constructed. They could be written as well as spoken and given as an aide memoir. Of course guidelines are not prescriptive. They need not be followed rigidly. They are a tool to help the learner. They can guide the learner through a new area that is complex for them. Once you have built two flat-pack bookcases you may be able to assemble the third without reference to the enclosed instruction sheet.

Teaching Tip

- Consider the use of guidelines as a teaching tool.

Summarising Your Teaching

> Therefore everyone who hears these words of mine and puts them into practice is like a wise man who builds his house on the rock. The rain came down, the streams rose, and the winds blew and beat upon that house; yet it did not fall, because it had its foundations on the rock. But everyone who hears these words of mine and does not put them into practice is like a foolish man who built his house on sand. The rain came down, the streams rose, and the winds blew and beat against that house, and it fell with a great crash.
>
> *Matthew 5:24-27*

Jesus summarises one hundred and two verses of teaching in four succinct verses. The summary took approximately four percent of the teaching time. That is a one minute summary for a twenty-five minute message. The summary is self explanatory but gripping in the sense it leaves the listener with a challenge........do you choose to follow Jesus' teaching or do you not?

The summary although factual also is emotional. It draws the listener into considering a personal choice. It is challenging and thought provoking. Jesus' message, spoken with authority, based on solid fact known to the listeners' leads to an ultimate choice. Which one will the listeners take? Indeed it is personal, as Jesus refers to the singular, "the man". The man is the listener. Does he/she resemble the wise man or the foolish one?

We have all sat through lectures and sermons where there does not appear to be a succinct conclusion or application. We have also sat though sermons where the conclusion takes as long as the main message; where the words "and now, finally" do not imply an impending ending, but more a heart sink to the listener, to know a further 20 minutes of summing up and duplication is to follow. Summaries should not introduce new ideas. They should draw all strands together and leave the listener in no doubt about the main point(s) of the talk. Jesus sets a good example; one twenty-fifth of teaching time is dedicated to the summary.

Constructing a good summary is an art that takes time and effort. How do you effectively encapsulate half an hour's teaching in one or two minutes? Part of the art is knowing what the aim(s) of the teaching was in the first place. The summary should reaffirm the aim and challenge and provoke the learner such that when they leave they will be more likely to remember what it was all about. For Jesus it was to make his followers 'wise' and blessed. They could choose to follow or not but the implications were explicit.

Teaching Tips

- Make the summary succinct.
- Personalise the summary.
- Make the summary thought provoking and challenging.

Evaluating Your Teaching

> When Jesus finished saying these things the crowds were amazed at his teaching, because he taught as one who had authority, and not as teachers of the law. When he came down from the mountainside, large crowds followed him.
>
> *Matthew 7:28 8:1*

Good teachers will always look for feedback. They seek some objective evidence that their teaching achieved its aims and was well received or not as the case may be, feedback can also be used to help the teacher know what they did well, or not so well. In academic circles a feedback form may be available to be completed by the listener. So was Jesus' teaching successful? How did Jesus gain feedback?

There can be no doubt that Jesus' teaching had produced the required reaction. He had an amazed audience many of whom continued to follow him. Jesus had objective evidence of the effects of his teaching. Not only could he, and others, see the faces of the learners but a good proportion chose to follow in the hope of hearing and learning more. As a teacher he could have thought, "Job well done".

We probably can all recall a teacher we had who was consistently bad and boring. A teacher who was set in their ways and never inspired as other teachers did. It was not just the topic but something more than that. The teaching techniques hindered rather than helped learning. Why did this teacher not change?

Feedback is not just about finding out what the listeners have learnt and how they felt about the learning experience. It is a means of helping us become better teachers. Criticism should be seen constructively to improve what we do. Of course it is hard to take criticism especially for those of us that are more sensitive than others.

When we teach, whether one individual or a crowd, it is unlikely we will experience the reaction of the crowd on the Mount. We do need to develop our own feedback tools. It may be that we would judge it a success if we were invited to take another teaching session. It may be we devise a simple questionnaire to be completed after the teaching event. It may be we simply ask the audience for feedback at the end of the session. No evaluation tool is perfect but it certainly is better than nothing! As they say, "If you don't ask you'll never know!"

Evaluation of effectiveness of teaching is not easy. It should also be remembered that evidence of what people do following a teaching session is more significant than what they say but is very much harder to ascertain.

Teaching Tips

- Try to think of ways to evaluate the effectiveness of your teaching
- Be prepared to take criticism.
- Try to see how your learners behave rather than just what they say.

Section 1: Teaching a Group Checklist

1. Establish a good teaching environment

Make sure you can be seen and heard well
Make sure your learners are comfortable

2. Cultivate motivated learners

Try to ensure the learners are motivated to listen and learn

3. Captivate your audience

Make sure the opening gains and holds the listeners' attention.
Have a personal application
Appeal to the self-interest of your audience

4. Personalise your message

Make the message applicable to each one present
Challenge each one

5. Build on prior knowledge

Build on the Listeners' Prior Knowledge
Establish what the learners know and build on it.

6. Speak with authority

Know your topic
Base any teaching on solid fact with references

7. Keep the listeners' attention

Fire challenging rhetorical questions to the audience

8. Give guidelines

Consider the use of guidelines as a useful aid for learners

9. End with a summary

Make the summary succinct
Make the summary thought provoking and challenging
Personalise the summary

10. Evaluate your teaching

Do not forget to evaluate the effectiveness of your teaching
Be prepared to take criticism

Section 2

Giving a Demonstration

One day as Jesus was standing by the Lake of Gennesaret, with the people crowding around him and listening to the word of God, he saw at the water's edge two boats, left there by the fishermen, who were washing their nets. He got into one of the boats, the one belonging to Simon, and asked him to put out a little from shore. Then he sat down and taught the people from the boat.

When he had finished speaking, he said to Simon, "Put out into deep water, and let down the nets for a catch."

Simon answered, "Master, we've worked hard all night and haven't caught anything. But because you say so, I will let down the nets."

When they had done so, they caught such a large number of fish that their nets began to break. So they signalled their partners in the other boat to come and help them, and they came and filled both boats so full that they began to sink.

When Simon Peter saw this, he fell at Jesus' knees and said, "Go away from me, Lord; I am a sinful man!" For he and all his companions were astonished at the catch of fish they had taken, and so were James and John, the sons of Zebedee, Simon's partners.

Then Jesus said to Simon, "Don't be afraid; from now on you will catch men." So they pulled their boats up on shore, left everything and followed him.

Luke 5: 1-11

Section 2: **Giving a Demonstration**

Actions speak louder than words, or so the saying goes. Another says that a picture is worth a thousand words. Seeing and experiencing something for yourself can have a bigger impact than just being told about it.

A magical moment for every father is being at the birth of your own child. No amount of reading or teaching can prepare you for the actual experience of being there and seeing it actually happening. In a way it is hard to believe the wonder without being there. No talk, video display or book comes anywhere close.

Jesus gave numerous demonstrations to his disciples and the people around. Rather than say something in words Jesus chose to let his followers see for themselves. His demonstrations revealed the wonder of God, his power and his spiritual truths. Some of these are very well known and include:

- The feeding of the five thousand
  (Matthew 14: 13-21; Mark 6:32-44; Luke9:10-17; John 6 1-13)
- Changing water into wine
  (John 2:3-9)

Right at the start of Jesus' ministry with his disciples he uses a powerful demonstration to teach them the purpose of their future work. Jesus is teaching a crowd but in addition he wants to show his first disciples something. It involves the letting down of nets to catch fish and is described in Luke 5: 1-11. This demonstration, to the individuals Jesus wishes to be his disciples, results in them following Him. Seeing results in them believing.

As teachers, by following Jesus' example, we can learn how to do demonstrations and make them most effective.

Having a Clear Aim

In carrying out a demonstration what do you want to achieve? What do you want people to see or experience? What are you wanting them to apply to their lives following this experience? Jesus carried out this demonstration with two aims in mind. Firstly, he was choosing his first disciples and wanted them to make a decision to follow him. Secondly, he wanted them to understand that their vocation would be to "catch men". How did he achieve this?

Before we carry out a demonstration we must be absolutely clear what the aim of the demonstration will be. What specifically are we trying to achieve? The aim will determine the nature of the demonstration.

Teaching Tip

- Have a clear aim

Being Seen and Heard

> One day as Jesus was standing by the Lake of Gennesaret, with the people crowding round him and listening to the word of God, he saw at the water's edge two boats, left there by the fishermen, who were washing their nets. *He got into one of the boats*, the one belonging to Simon, and asked him *to put out a little from shore*. Then *he sat down* and taught the people from the boat.
>
> *Luke 5:1-3*

Have you ever been to the theatre, sports fixture or an event requiring you to watch a demonstration and had a seat with a bad view so you could not fully see what was happening? Have you ever sat through a demonstration where you could not hear properly? Not being able to see or hear fully will have an impact on learning. You need to give thought to preparing the 'stage' for the demonstration so that the listeners can see and hear well.

Jesus planned where best to position himself to give a demonstration to a large number of people; a place where they could see and hear. Being in a boat, a little off the shore was the perfect location.

Teaching Tip

- Make sure the audience can both see and hear.

Being Clear in Your Instructions

> When he had finished speaking, he said to Simon, "*Put out* into *deep water* and *let down* the nets for a catch".
>
> *Luke 5: 4*

For a demonstration to have its best impact, the learner must appreciate what is happening. The teacher needs to describe what to do, breaking it down to its basic steps or movements. You need to remember that what is easy and comprehensible to you may not be to your learners. It is best to keep things as simple as possible, including the instructions.

One potential pitfall to avoid is that of selecting an inappropriate helper. What is required of the helper should be understandable and possible by them. I have experienced embarrassing moments when a visiting preacher has selected a 'willing' child volunteer from the congregation to carry out sophisticated movements and verbal tasks. The child unfortunately did not have the understanding to carry out the tasks required disrupting the demonstration and causing embarrassment. The message is to know and pre-select any helper.

Jesus gives instructions to Simon which are clear, succinct and precise. Simon, the learner could be in no doubt what to do and what was expected. As a fisherman the tasks were very familiar to him.

Step 1: Put out into deep water
Step 2: Let down the nets to catch fish

Teaching Tips

- Give instructions which are precise and clear.
- Know your helper

Involving the Learner

When he had finished speaking, *he said to Simon*, "*(You, Simon),* Put out into deep water and let down the nets for a catch".

Luke 5: 4

Why did Jesus not go out alone and let down the nets himself? Why did he ask Simon, hid student, to carry out the instructions?

The evidence is that people learn better if they achieve something for themselves rather than just being passive observers. Simon would never forget the demonstration. He would also remember the end result, achieved by himself, not by the teacher. The audience would also be more interested because an ordinary person was included too.

Teaching Tip

- Involve the learner in the demonstration.

Encouraging Audience Participation

> Simon answered, "Master, we've worked hard all night and haven't caught anything. But because you say so, I will let down the nets".
>
> *Luke 5:5*

Demonstrations are meant to stimulate and challenge the observer(s). People learn better if they are able to actively participate in the demonstration by asking questions or commenting. Jesus delivered his demonstration such that he knew it would challenge Simon. Jesus wanted his pupil to see for himself. That way he would fully believe what had happened.

Simon was an experienced fisherman. He was implicitly questioning the worth of the demonstration based on his own worldly experience. The demonstration would give Simon in particular and the wider audience in general, the chance to have an 'awesome experience.' Simon would see first hand evidence of what he had not been able to achieve and what was possible with God. In his judgement putting down nets to catch fish would be futile. He voiced his disquiet and reservations.

Jesus as the teacher did not immediately jump in with a retort to explain to Simon how wrong he would be. The demonstration was to show Simon the truth about Jesus. The result of the demonstration would speak. Jesus' respected Simon's comments and allowed Simon to carry on. He acknowledged that Simon would see for himself.

Teaching Tips

- Encourage and respect learner participation
- Allow the demonstration to 'speak' for itself!

Making Sure the Audience Can See

> ….they caught such a large number of fish, that their nets began to break. So they *(Jesus and Simon)* signalled to their partners in the other boat to come and help them, and they came and filled both boats so full that they began to sink.
>
> *Luke 5: 6-7*

In this demonstration Jesus appears to be directing his demonstration at several audiences. Firstly Jesus chose Simon to be closest to the action. Indeed he chose Simon to carry out the demonstration following his instructions. Secondly he chose to involve Simon's fishing partners, James and John. Indeed they saw and experienced first hand the result of the demonstration. Thirdly, the wider audience viewing the demonstration from the lakeshore would see what was happening. They would appreciate from the fishermen's activity that a great many fish were caught. They would see not only the fishermen working; they would also see the boat settled lower in the water from the weight of the catch.

In giving a demonstration we need to be clear who our main audience is. Is the demonstration specifically aimed at one individual? Are there a group of people you wish to be closer to the action? Is the demonstration equally relevant to all? In the first scenario it may be best to have the individual as the 'helper'. In the second the targeted group could be positioned nearest to the action through appropriate seating. In the third scenario the most important thing is to have the demonstration seen and heard by all equally.

Teaching Tip

- Be clear who your main audience is and whom you wish to influence most.

Evaluating the Impact of the Demonstration

> When Simon Peter saw this, he fell at Jesus' knees and said," Go away from me, Lord; I am a sinful man!" For he and all his companions were astonished at the catch of fish they had taken, and so were James and John, the sons of Zebedee, Simon's partners.
>
> Then Jesus said to Simon, "Don't be afraid; from now on you will catch men."
>
> So they pulled their boats up on shore, left everything and followed him.
>
> Luke 5:8-11

Good teachers will always look for objective evidence that their teaching methods achieve their aims and are well received. So was Jesus' demonstration successful? Did he achieve his aims? How did Jesus gain his feedback?

There are numerous ways to evaluate the impact of a demonstration. These include verbal feedback, personal observation and the behavioural response of the observers. As a teacher you need to decide how you will know objectively that your demonstration has been effective. Feeling something has gone well and believing you have done well although producing a warm glow inside and being personally reassuring is not objective enough.

Jesus had objective evidence of the impact of his demonstration through several means:

Visual and Verbal feedback

Simon gave his feedback spontaneously to Jesus by falling on his knees acknowledging Jesus as Lord and stating his acknowledgement of his own sinfulness.

Personal Observation

Jesus could see for himself the astonishment on the faces of his learners.

Behavioural response

We are told Simon and his partners left everything and followed Jesus. His demonstration had resulted in these men giving their all.

Teaching Tips

- Evaluate the impact of your demonstration
- Listen to what is said, observe how people look and watch how they may behave.

Finishing with a Word of Encouragement.

> Then Jesus said to Simon, "*Don't be afraid*; from now on you will catch men."
>
> So they pulled their boats up on shore, left everything and followed him.
> *Luke 10 b*

Jesus did not just finish with a fact or by reiterating the result of the demonstration. He responded to the feelings of the disciples in an encouraging supportive way. Jesus sought not only to impart knowledge but also to give wisdom and precipitate action. He wants us to do something in response to learning a spiritual truth and not just know something. This involves not just the 'head' but the 'heart'.

Taking new steps in life can often lead to 'fear'. Jesus was very aware of this and addressed the specific emotional implications of his demonstration. He responded to how the disciples were feeling after the demonstration. He anticipated their fear and sensitively responded to it.

Remember we are giving a demonstration with a specific aim in mind. The demonstration will hopefully reveal some new truth to the observer(s). The outcome could have quite a profound effect, particularly on the helper but also to any observer. It is important to finish the demonstration with words of encouragement for the observers to allow them to make the practical changes to their lives in response to the new knowledge.

Teaching Tips

- Be aware of the potential emotional impact of your demonstration
- Give a word of encouragement to your learners to give them confidence and ease any 'fear'.

Section 2: Giving a Demonstration Checklist

1. **Have a clear aim**

2. **Make sure you can be seen and heard**

3. **Give clear instructions**
   Give instructions which are precise and clear
   Know your helper(s)

4. **Involve the learner(s)**
   If possible let the learner(s) do the demonstration

5. **Encourage audience participation**
   Encourage and respect learner participation

6. **Make sure audience see results of demonstration**
   Be clear who your main audience is

7. **Evaluate the impact of the demonstration**
   Listen to what is said, observe how people look and watch how they may behave.

8. **Finish with a word of encouragement**
   Be aware of the emotional impact of your demonstration
   Give encouragement to give the learners confidence

Section 3

Using a Case Study

The Widow's Offering

Jesus sat down opposite the place where the offerings were put and watched the crowd putting their money into the temple treasury. Many rich people threw in large amounts. But a poor widow came and put in two very small copper coins, worth only a fraction of a penny.

Calling his disciples to him, Jesus said, "I tell you the truth, this poor widow has put more into the treasury than all the others. They all gave out of their wealth; but she, out of her poverty, put in everything–all she had to live on."

Mark 12:41-44

Section 3: **Using a Case Study**

In training to be a doctor I remember the way I was taught by the trainer at the patient's bedside. This was about real life and in real time. The text book knowledge about conditions, signs and symptoms could be seen 'in the flesh'. Medical theoretical and academic knowledge were made to apply in everyday life. The patient was the 'case' and the medical student was asked to observe and examine. It allows the actual detail to be seen and appreciated. Seeing a patient is an everyday event in the life of a doctor. Remembering the lessons of case studies is a cornerstone of being better able to diagnose and treat illness.

In a similar way an everyday or notable occurrence can be used as a case study. It can teach a principal or illustrate a point to a learner or group of learners. The head knowledge can be applied to this situation. The situation will illustrate and draw out vividly and practically the lessons to be learnt. Being in the same situation again may trigger recollection of the lesson.

Three examples of events which happened to Jesus and his disciples in the course of their daily ministry and which Jesus used to powerfully teach them deep spiritual truths are:

1. **The Rich Young Man:** *A chance occurrence*
   (Mark 10:17-31, Matthew 19:16-30, Luke 18: 18-30)

Jesus uses a chance encounter with a rich man asking about eternal life to explain to his disciples that eternal life is impossible to achieve through human means but is entirely possible through God.

2. The Little Children and Jesus : *A familiar occurrence*
    (Mark 10:13 -16, Matthew 19: 13-15, Luke 18: 15-17)

After the disciples try to deter people from bringing their children to Jesus, he points out that the kingdom of God belongs to those with child –like attributes who receive the kingdom of God simply as a free gift.

3. The Widow's Offering : *A regular occurrence*
    (Mark 12:41-44, Luke 21:1-4)

An observation of people giving their offerings in the temple enables Jesus to show that it is not the earthly value of a gift which is of value to God but rather the sacrifice the giver makes to God in what he or she gives.

Choosing a Familiar Case

> Jesus sat down opposite the place where the offerings were put and watched the crowd putting their money into the temple treasury. Many rich people threw in large amounts. But a poor widow came and put in two very small copper coins, worth only a fraction of a penny.
>
> *Mark 12: 41-42*

Jesus was with his disciples in the temple. This was a regular occurrence and a very familiar situation. Jesus had positioned them such that they were observing individuals put money into one of the thirteen trumpet-shaped receptacles used to collect the contributions. He uses this everyday familiar event to illustrate to the disciples that giving is about the heart and sacrifice, not status and standing.

Jesus drew to the attention of the disciples the way the rich people threw in their large amounts of coins, in contrast to a poor widow who put in a very small amount. Jesus has chosen a case study illustrating extreme positions to make the emphasis obvious to his disciples. The rich people had an outward show of extravagance which was seen by all and on the face of it cost them very little. In contrast the widow placed her coins carefully and privately into the receptacle. There was no outward show and in worldly terms the offering cost her a great deal.

One of the main benefits of this technique is that there is a real chance that every time the disciples were in the same situation they would remember the teaching and the spiritual truth. It provides a means of reinforcing learning. They could also teach it to others.

To be effective at using this technique the teacher needs to be perceptive at observing and seeing the spiritual truths in everyday events. In a way it requires looking through spiritual eyes at each circumstance to view its spiritual relevance for teaching.

Teaching Tips

- Use everyday events to illustrate a spiritual truth
- Make the case relevant, topical and straightforward

Involving the Learners at the Time

> *Calling his disciples to him*, Jesus said," I tell you the truth, this poor widow has put more into the treasury than all the others. They all gave out of their wealth; but she, out of her poverty, put in everything – all she had to live on".
>
> *Mark 12: 43-44*

Jesus brings his disciples to reflect on this real life situation at the time it happened. He does not wait to talk about this at a later time. The best impact of a case study is by it being immediately available as a teaching tool. He made sure the case study was topical, relevant and straightforward. The disciples would be able to identify with it. They could immediately apply the principle Jesus wished to teach.

Teaching Tip

- Make your point(s) there and then

Guiding the Learners to Apply the Case Study

> Calling his disciples to him, *Jesus said,"* I tell you the truth, this poor widow has put more into the treasury than all the others. They all gave out of their wealth; but she, out of her poverty, put in everything – all she had to live on".
>
> Mark 12: 43-44

It is good educational practice to provide a succinct summary at the end of each period of teaching. The summary reinforces the prior learning. Learners will leave with the summary ringing in their ears.

Jesus could simply have given didactic 'classroom' talk on the principles of Christian giving. However Jesus chose to reveal the principles using an observation at the Temple. Following the observation Jesus summed up the spiritual truth. He provided a summary. The disciples were not left with just words, however. They were left with a vivid image that would be repeated again and again each time they attended the temple and noticed the giving.

Teaching Tips

- Make the case relevant, topical and straightforward
- Get to the heart of the issue by outlining the principles involved.
- Allow reflection and discussion
- Reinforce the message

Section 3 : **Using a Case Study Checklist**

1. **Choose a case well known to the learners**
   Everyday events can be used to illustrate spiritual truths
   Make the case relevant, topical and straightforward

2. **Involve the learners at the time of the event/ case**
   Make your point there and then

3. **Guide the learners to apply the case study** *Draw out key points from the observation*
   Allow reflection and discussion
   Get to the heart of the issue by outlining the principles involved

4. **Reinforce the message**

Section 4

Using an Allegory or Parable (Story)

The disciples came to him and asked, "Why do you speak to the people in parables?"
He replied, "The knowledge of the secrets of the kingdom of heaven has been given to you, but not to them. Whoever has will be given more, and he will have an abundance. Whoever does not have, even what he has will be taken from him. This is why I speak to them in parables: "Though seeing, they do not see; though hearing, they do not hear or understand.
In them is fulfilled the prophecy of Isaiah:
" 'You will be ever hearing but never understanding;
you will be ever seeing but never perceiving.
For this people's heart has become calloused;
they hardly hear with their ears,
and they have closed their eyes.
Otherwise they might see with their eyes,
hear with their ears,
understand with their hearts
and turn, and I would heal them.'
"But blessed are your eyes because they see, and your ears because they hear. For I tell you the truth, many prophets and righteous men longed to see what you see but did not see it, and to hear what you hear but did not hear it."

Matthew 13: 1-17

The Parables of the Mustard Seed and the Yeast
He told them another parable: "The kingdom of heaven is like a mustard seed, which a man took and planted in his field. Though it is the smallest

of all your seeds, yet when it grows, it is the largest of garden plants and becomes a tree, so that the birds of the air come and perch in its branches."

He told them still another parable: "The kingdom of heaven is like yeast that a woman took and mixed into a large amount of flour until it worked all through the dough."

Jesus spoke all these things to the crowd in parables; he did not say anything to them without using a parable. So was fulfilled what was spoken through the prophet: "I will open my mouth in parables, I will utter things hidden since the creation of the world."

Matthew 13: 31 -35

Section 4: **Using an Allegory or Parable**

Sometimes stories and allegories can be used to illustrate a truth or principle. A parable or allegory is a story or image which is understood symbolically. Jesus told many stories. His parables are well known. Parables and allegories are different to case studies because they are not necessarily actual events that happened.

One of the recognised ways to help people learn is to build on their current knowledge or experience. This places learning in context and moves the learners' understanding forward. A story or allegory drawing on the listeners' prior knowledge or understanding can help them understand better.

Jesus used parables to illustrate *spiritual* truths or principles to his listeners. Why did he choose this teaching method?

> *"This is why* I speak to them in parables:
> Though seeing, they do not see;
> Though hearing, they do not hear or understand".
>
> *Matthew 13:13*

As a child I loved to hear Aesop's fables. Seemingly they are simple children's stories but used to illustrate deep truths that are pertinent to adults. The short stories helped me understand in a simple way matters that for a child were very profound and complex. Forty years later I still apply the lesson of the hare and the tortoise in my everyday management. I know that being slow yet steady can produce end results quicker than by very rapid short bursts with rests or distractions in between.

People in Jesus' time were not learning spiritual truths from the regular ways of being taught; through seeing or hearing. There was a spiritual dullness in the people. Jesus used parables as a particular teaching tool for a particular reason; to challenge the learners' spiritual being and understanding. Speaking in parables allowed some of them to grasp the spiritual message.

The apparent vagueness of the parable or allegory caused the listeners to think, reflect and discuss. It is well known that discussion and argument can lead to deeper learning. This method was not effective in all listeners; some still could not understand, or chose not to apply the principles outlined in the story.

Keeping the Stories Short

The Parables of the Mustard Seed and the Yeast

He told them another parable: "The kingdom of heaven is like a mustard seed, which a man took and planted in his field. Though it is the smallest of all your seeds, yet when it grows, it is the largest of garden plants and becomes a tree, so that the birds of the air come and perch in its branches."

He told them still another parable: "The kingdom of heaven is like yeast that a woman took and mixed into a large amount of flour until it worked all through the dough."

Matthew 13:31-33

I remember the advert well. "Win a Luxury holiday!" it said. What I and other readers were invited to do was answer a particular question and state in up to 30 words, "I would like to go on holiday because…….. Thirty words only. For me I needed to write a detailed essay. How do I encapsulate all my thoughts, feelings and hopes in so few words? The answer is , "with great difficulty", but it can be done. It took me a great deal of thought and time but the end product was a distillation of my key thoughts producing a very succinct, focussed message.

An allegory is a story which to be remembered and applied by the learner must be short, interesting and relevant. People will not remember or be stimulated to apply lessons from long dull stories. A complex truth needs to be distilled into simple language using few but sufficient words.

The two parables of the mustard seed and yeast are told by Jesus in three consecutive verses which in translation are less than one hundred words. The allegories although very short are very much focussed to address their objective. Their brevity and relevance helps them to be remembered in their entirety by the listeners.

Teaching Tip

- Keep the story short and to the point

Building on Previous Understanding

> He told them another parable: "The kingdom of heaven is like a mustard seed, which a man took and planted in his field. Though it is the smallest of all your seeds, yet when it grows, it is the largest of garden plants and becomes a tree, so that the birds of the air come and perch in its branches."
>
> He told them still another parable: "The kingdom of heaven is like yeast that a woman took and mixed into a large amount of flour until it worked all through the dough."
>
> *Matthew 13:31-33*

The stories used illustrations that would be very familiar to the listeners for two main reasons. Firstly, in the society of the day would they be a normal part of everyday life. The learners would relate to both the agricultural and domestic scenarios involving the planting of mustard seeds and the use of yeast. Secondly, the Jews would be aware of Old Testament teachings and stories. In these two parables Jesus carefully draws upon scriptures from the Old Testament.

The Birds perching in branches occurs in Psalm 104 and the books of Ezekiel and Daniel.

- The birds of the air nest by the waters; they sing among the branches
  Psalm 104:12

- "…..it will produce branches…..Birds of every kind will nest in it; they will find shelter in the shade of its branches."
  Ezekiel 17: 23

- "The tree grew large and strong...... and the birds of the air lived in its branches...."
  Daniel 4:12

The picture of the woman taking flour would evoke memories of the story of the three visitors coming to Abraham who wished to give them something to eat as recounted in the book of Genesis.

- So Abraham hurried into the tent to Sarah. "Quick", he said," get the three seahs of fine flour and knead it and bake some bread."
  Genesis 18:6

Drawing on common everyday experience and knowledge of current teachings Jesus constructed his parables to be easily remembered and spiritually applied in the lives of those who reflected on them.

Teaching Tip

- Construct stories that draw on common experience and common knowledge

Making the Story Believable

Jesus made his parables believable. The listeners would see they could be real situations. Whether it is the parable of the Mustard Seed, Yeast, the Sower *(Matthew 13:1-15)*, the Net *(Matthew 13: 47-50)*, the Hidden Treasure *(Matthew 13: 44)* or the Pearl *(Matthew 13:45)* the listeners could imagine the situation as happening in real life. It was a believable scenario.

Teaching Tip

- Make the story believable

Making the Story Personal

> He told them another parable: "The kingdom of heaven is like a mustard seed, which a man took and planted in his field. Though it is the smallest of all your seeds, yet when it grows, it is the largest of garden plants and becomes a tree, so that the birds of the air come and perch in its branches."
>
> *Matthew 13: 31-32*

Have you ever sat in a congregation and felt the message given by the preacher was directed at you? When you have come out of church you have said to a friend" I thought he or she *(the preacher)* was talking to me!" If so you will appreciate that hearing a personal message makes you sit up and listen. A message or lecture directed specifically at the listener is more likely to be remembered and have an impact.

Jesus personalises the parable by making the listeners a part of the story. This was not any mustard seed; this was a mustard seed that belonged to the listeners. The story was made directly applicable to each of them.

Teaching Tip

- Make the story personally applicable to each listener

Ending with a Challenge

"This is why I speak to them in parables:

Though seeing, they do not see;

Though hearing, they do not hear or understand".

He told them another parable: "The kingdom of heaven is like a mustard seed, which a man took and planted in his field. Though it is the smallest of all your seeds, yet when it grows, it is the largest of garden plants and becomes a tree, so that the birds of the air come and perch in its branches."

He who has ears, let him hear.

Matthew 13: 13, 31-32,43b

Another teaching tactic of Jesus is to challenge his listeners directly after telling a parable. Jesus in answer to the disciples' question explained to them why he spoke in parables. He then told them a few parables. At the end he challenged them to 'hear' what he was saying; to understand the spiritual truth encapsulated in the story. After the parable of the Sower Jesus provides the direct personal challenge" "He who has ears, let him hear." *(Matthew 13:9, Mark 4:9).* There was no avoiding the fact that the story was aimed to challenge the listener personally.

Teaching Tip

- End a story with a personal challenge to the listener

Section 4: **Using an Allegory or Parable Checklist**

1. Keep the story short and to the point
2. Build on previous knowledge or understanding
3. Make the story believable
4. Make the story personal to each listener
5. End with a challenge personal to each listener

Section 5

Being a Mentor

When Jesus came to the region of Caesarea Philippi, he asked his disciples, "Who do people say the Son of Man is?"

They replied, "Some say John the Baptist; others say Elijah; and still others, Jeremiah or one of the prophets."

"But what about you?" he asked. "Who do you say I am?"

Simon Peter answered, "You are the Christ, the Son of the living God."

Jesus replied, "Blessed are you, Simon son of Jonah, for this was not revealed to you by man, but by my Father in heaven.

Matthew 16: 13 -17

Section 5: **Being a Mentor**

A mentor is a wise councillor. In the context of teaching it is someone who develops a learning relationship with a learner or group of learners to help them reach their potential through a process of reflective practice. Reflection implies meditating and thinking about a subject to reach one's own conclusion. The mentor helps stimulate this process.

There is no doubt that throughout Jesus' ministry he formed a close bond with his disciples. The root of the word disciple means 'one who professes to receive instruction from another' (Chambers Dictionary). The bond Jesus formed with his disciples was not just master and follower but also respected teacher and willing learner. The disciples followed Jesus wanting to learn. Jesus took a particular interest in them, cultivating their learning. He became their mentor.

A didactic teacher will tell students what he or she wants them to know. Whether the student believes it, remembers it or understands it is another matter. A wise teacher will at some point try to tease out what a student does think and believe, supporting and encouraging them in the process. Jesus did not just tell his disciples things. He made them think and reflect. He was interested to know what they thought. He wanted them to think for themselves, to form their own opinions and therefore be convinced of the truth.

Asking Probing Questions

> When Jesus came to the region of Caesar Philippi, *he asked* his disciples, "Who do people say the son of man is?"
>
> They replied, "Some say John the Baptist, others say Elijah; and still others, Jeremiah or one of the prophets."
>
> "But what about you?" *he asked*, "Who do you say I am?"
>
> Simon Peter answered, "You are the Christ, the Son of the living God."
>
> Jesus replied, "Blessed are you, Simon son of Jonah, for this was not revealed to you by man but by my Father in heaven".
>
> Matthew 16 13-17

Jesus, after several years mentoring his disciples chose to ask them who people and more specifically they, thought he was. Would they know the spiritual truth? As their mentor he asked them directly. He asked them what their personal view was despite what others may say. Their answer could only have come from their personal experience of knowing Jesus and it represented what they truly believed. Simon Peter gave the answer with conviction that recognised Jesus as God's Son. Words had not been put in his mouth. Jesus had not previously told him who he was. Simon Peter had arrived at this conclusion following his own period of reflection on what had gone before. By blessing him Jesus affirmed that Simon Peter's answer was correct.

Mentoring Tip

- Ask direct questions to establish what mentees know or believe.

Helping Resolve Arguments

> An argument started among the disciples as to which of them would be the greatest. Jesus, knowing their thoughts, took a little child and made him stand beside him. Then he said to them, "Whoever welcomes this little child in my name welcomes me; and whoever welcomes me welcomes the one who sent me. For he who is least among you all – he is the greatest."
>
> *Luke 9:46-48*

A good mentor will be an excellent listener. S/he will understand what is making the mentees tick. In this case Jesus was listening to the disciples argue. Through listening to the argument he knew what they were thinking. He did not immediately interrupt and didactically tell them the answer. He did not confront argument with further argument. He needed them to come to their own conclusions. To do this he enlisted the help of a child. In a masterly way Jesus challenged their reasoning of worldly greatness by confronting them with the child-like characteristics they would need to assume to become spiritually great.

Jesus did not enter the argument. He did not resort to forcing his views on the disciples. He made them confront their differences and confusion in a calm constructive way. He helped them see for themselves the solution to resolve their argument.

Mentoring Tips

- Listen and understand what any argument is about
- Do not enter the argument with your own argument.
- Guide the learners to come to their own solution.

Comforting through Difficult Times

> On the evening of that first day of the week, when the disciples were together, with the doors locked for fear of the Jews, Jesus came and stood among them and said, "Peace be with you!" After he said this, he showed them his hands and side. The disciples were overjoyed when they saw the lord.
>
> John 20: 19-20

I remember as a very young child being afraid of the dark. Alone in my bedroom I worried about 'the bogeyman'. Shutting my bedroom door was no comfort. Having my father tell me that I 'had nothing to be afraid of' before going to bed helped a little. What gave me the greatest comfort was mum or dad actually coming into the darkness of my bedroom to give me a reassuring, "Good-night" and a kiss. Fears about the bogeyman instantly receded.

The disciples could not have been in more need of comfort. Things could not have appeared darker. They had lost their leader and purpose for living. In addition they were in mortal danger from fellow Jews. Jesus came to be among them in this bleak situation. He did not send a note or a verbal message via another person. He appeared in person. Reaffirming that he indeed had overcome death and thereby showing that his spiritual teachings were true he restored to the disciples their purpose and hope. Jesus' presence helped them overcome their fear and indeed filled them with joy.

As teachers our students will have times when they need comfort. They may need help in grasping and holding on to spiritual truths when times get tough is. As mentors we need to be sensitive to when our students are feeling low or helpless. We need to be sensitive to times when they are struggling to grasp that the spiritual truths apply in every situation no matter how awkward and hopeless it appears. What students will appreciate is the mentor personally coming among them and offering support.

Mentoring Tips

- Comfort students when necessary.
- Wherever possible do it in person.

Praying for Your Students

After Jesus said this, he looked towards heaven and prayed:

> "Now they know that everything you have given me comes from you. For I gave them the words you gave me and they accepted them. They knew with certainty that I came from you, and they believed that you sent me. I pray for them. I am not praying for the world, but for those you have given me, for they are yours. All I have is yours, and all you have is mine. And glory has come to me through them. I will remain in the world no longer, but they are still in the world, and I am coming to you. Holy Father, protect them by the power of your name - the name you gave me - so that they might be one as we are one.
>
> *John 17: 1, 7-11*

Prayer is an integral part of our Christian life. Through prayer we know a personal relationship with Jesus Christ. In prayer we can bring to Jesus things that are important to us, whether it is to say thank-you, to acknowledge God's goodness or to pray for situations and people with particular needs. As teachers, in our prayers, we need to remember the responsibility we have to our students and how special they are.

Jesus cared about the welfare of his disciples. He took time to pray for them, committing them and their future work to his Father. It is very easy as teachers and mentors to only care for students when in their presence. Jesus gladly took his work home. Teaching was a vocation not a job. Teaching and caring for his disciples was an integral part of his life. He knew the importance of surrounding his teaching and his students with prayer. He directly prayed for himself and his disciples. As Jesus prayed for his students so we should pray for ours.

Mentoring Tips

- Surround your teaching with prayer
- Pray for your students.

Section 5 : **Mentoring Checklist**

1. **Be a good listener**
   Try to understand what is being said

2. **Ask probing questions**
   Ask direct questions to establish what students know or believe

3. **Help resolve and arguments or disputes**
   Listen and understand the reason for the argument
   Do not confront the argument with your own argument
   Guide the learner to come to their own resolution

4. **Comfort in difficult times**
   Comfort students when necessary
   Do it in person

5. **Pray for your students**
   Surround your teaching with prayer
   Pray for your students

Section 6

Setting a Practical Project

Jesus Sends Out the Twelve

When Jesus had called the Twelve together, he gave them power and authority to drive out all demons and to cure diseases, and he sent them out to preach the kingdom of God and to heal the sick. He told them: "Take nothing for the journey—no staff, no bag, no bread, no money, no extra tunic. Whatever house you enter, stay there until you leave that town. If people do not welcome you, shake the dust off your feet when you leave their town, as a testimony against them." So they set out and went from village to village, preaching the gospel and healing people everywhere.

When the apostles returned, they reported to Jesus what they had done. Then he took them with him and they withdrew by themselves to a town called Bethsaida,

Luke 9: 1-6, 10

Section 6: **Setting a Practical Project**

> When Jesus had called the Twelve together, he gave them power and authority to drive out all demons and to cure diseases, and he sent them out to preach the kingdom of God and to heal the sick. He told them: "take nothing for the journey – no staff, no bag, no bread, no money, no extra tunic. Whatever house you enter stay there until you leave that town. If people do not welcome you, shake the dust off your feet when you leave their town, as a testimony against them.
>
> When the apostles returned, they reported to Jesus what they had done. Then he took them with him and they withdrew by themselves to a town called Bethsaida.
>
> *Luke 9:1-6, 10*

In vocational training there comes a point when the theory you have learnt has to be applied in the real world. Reading all the technical books on plumbing will not make you a competent plumber. Watching someone else do it will also not make you competent. You have to do it yourself to prove the value of the teaching and gain competence and confidence. The same is true of being a good teacher. You learn teaching theory, you observe other teachers teaching and then you have to undertake classroom teaching practice.

Jesus has taught his disciples many truths. He has shown them many things and they have observed Jesus at work. The next step in their training was for them to apply what they had learnt and do it for themselves. Jesus set them a practical project. He sent them out to preach and heal. He is encouraging his disciples to carry out the ministry he had trained them to follow.

As a teacher Jesus planned the project very carefully. In this passage we see Jesus carrying out three main elements of (i) induction, (ii) instruction and (iii) debriefing.

Giving an Induction

> When Jesus had called the Twelve together, he gave them power and authority to drive out all demons and to cure diseases,
>
> *Luke 9:1*

The word authority given in the scripture has as the root of its meaning that of being given a privilege or licence to practice. In essence it implies the disciples had passed the test and were qualified to practice – in the view of their teacher. Jesus called them all to a spiritual awards ceremony bestowing on them affirmation of their qualification to practice.

Some years ago Kim, my wife was learning to fly. This involved many hours of bookwork learning flying theory accompanied by supervised flying practice. The time had arrived when the instructor made the judgement that Kim could fly solo. In his assessment Kim was competent and able. He relayed this to Kim and the solo flight was booked. She had his authority and backing despite the doubts she herself felt in her own ability. The flight instruction was given and a first solo flight was competently accomplished. Would Kim have attempted a solo flight if her personal instructor, the one who had trained her, had not confidently said she was able? I doubt not.

Jesus called his disciples together before they embarked on their first solo mission. He made sure they were equipped for the task in hand. They had passed the test. Jesus, their instructor personally told them they were qualified and ready. He believed in their ability and personally gave them his authority to proceed.

Teaching Tips

- Ensure the student is qualified and adequately trained to carry out the project.
- Take personal interest in telling the students they are 'able'.

Giving Instructions

> He told them: "take nothing for the journey – no staff, no bag, no bread, no money, no extra tunic. Whatever house you enter stay there until you leave that town. If people do not welcome you, shake the dust off your feet when you leave their town, as a testimony against them
>
> *Luke 9: 3-5*

Parents, you will all remember your child's first day at school and the instructions you gave. "Take this, don't take that, remember your packed lunch, have a little money in case and listen to the teachers!" The instructions made clear what was required. It ensured the child was properly prepared for the experience of the new challenge ahead.

In the same way Jesus gave specific instructions to his disciples to ensure they were adequately equipped for their first mission. They were also instructed how to behave among the community in which they chose to minister.

Teaching Tip

- Give clear instructions

Carrying out a Debriefing

> When the apostles returned, they reported to Jesus what they had done. Then he took them with him and they withdrew by themselves to a town called Bethsaida.
>
> *Luke 9: 10*

It is essential following a practical test to evaluate how well or badly it had gone. This allows the learner and teacher to review the good and not so good areas of practice and make any necessary changes so that if repeated the project can be better accomplished. A debriefing should be an essential part of the learning process. As such it should be given the time it deserves and not rushed.

Jesus made time to listen to his disciples' report. He made time and practical preparation to share time with them. Indeed it appears he had planned a retreat with them.

Teaching Tip

- Make time and practical arrangements for a debriefing.

Section 6: **Setting a Practical Project Checklist**

1. **Have an induction period**
   Ensure the students are adequately trained and qualified
   Take a personal interest in telling students they are 'able'

2. **Give Instructions**
   Give clear instructions

3. **Carry out a debriefing**
   Make time and practical arrangements for a debriefing

Section 7

Qualities of a Christian Teacher

You must teach what is in accord with sound doctrine. Teach the older men to be temperate, worthy of respect, self-controlled, and sound in faith, in love and in endurance.

Likewise, teach the older women to be reverent in the way they live, not to be slanderers or addicted to much wine, but to teach what is good. Then they can train the younger women to love their husbands and children, to be self-controlled and pure, to be busy at home, to be kind, and to be subject to their husbands, so that no one will malign the word of God.

Similarly, encourage the young men to be self-controlled. In everything set them an example by doing what is good. In your teaching show integrity, seriousness and soundness of speech that cannot be condemned, so that those who oppose you may be ashamed because they have nothing bad to say about us.

Teach slaves to be subject to their masters in everything, to try to please them, not to talk back to them, and not to steal from them, but to show that they can be fully trusted, so that in every way they will make the teaching about God our Saviour attractive.

For the grace of God that brings salvation has appeared to all men. It teaches us to say "No" to ungodliness and worldly passions, and to live self-controlled, upright and godly lives in this present age, while we wait for the blessed hope—the glorious appearing of our great God and Saviour, Jesus Christ, who gave himself for us to redeem us from all wickedness and to purify for himself a people that are his very own, eager to do what is good.

These, then, are the things you should teach. Encourage and rebuke with all authority. Do not let anyone despise you.

Titus 2: 1-15

Section 7: Qualities of a Christian Teacher

What makes a good teacher? I am sure that we can all recall at least one teacher from our days in education who we viewed as someone special; a teacher who inspired us and perhaps influenced our lives. If we thought about the particular qualities that made this teacher special to us we may identify some or all of the following traits:

- Enthusiasm
- Friendliness
- Interest in students
- Competence
- Knowledge
- Confidence
- Charisma
- Willingness to prepare well
- Patience
- Ability to listen

The following news headline is one that that vividly illustrates that there is a world of difference between being able to technically teach well and being a good teacher.

A teacher from XXXXX has been charged with sexual offences against children.

The teacher may have had a good teaching technique and been able to teach well. S/he may have been the most gifted at applying teaching theory. Was s/he a good teacher? Of course not. S/he will have lost all respect and the trust of fellow teachers, pupils and parents as well as wider society. The missing ingredient was the integrity of character. This stark example illustrates vividly that teaching is not just about technical ability; it is also about our character.

Requirements of Christian Teachers

In the New Testament the book of Titus includes a section on teaching. It draws out some of the attributes needed to be a Christian teacher.

> You must teach what is in accord with *sound doctrine*......In everything *set them an example* by *doing what is good*. In your teaching *show integrity, seriousness and soundness of speech* that cannot be condemned, so that those who oppose you may be ashamed because they have nothing bad to say about us......For the grace of God that brings salvation has appeared to all men. It teaches us to *say "No" to ungodliness and worldly passions* and to *live self –controlled, upright and godly lives* in this present age.....*Encourage and rebuke* with all authority. *Do not let anyone despise you.*
>
> Titus 2: 1, 7, 8, 11, 12,15b

The requirements of us are to:

- Become an example to the people we teach
- Teach sound doctrine
- Show integrity
- Show appropriate seriousness
- Have sound teaching
- Say "No" to ungodliness
- Say "No" to worldly passions
- Live self controlled lives
- Be upright and godly
- Encourage
- Rebuke
- Not do anything which will make us be despised

As teachers working to deliver God's message, we need to understand the responsibility placed upon each one of us. Not only must we work to improve our teaching techniques. In parallel we must work to improve the integrity of our lives. As teachers we do not turn up to give a one hour lecture. We are 'on show' twenty four hours a day. What we do outside face to face teaching also reflects directly on our standing as teachers. We can not be good teachers of God's word if our lives do not reflect what we believe and are teaching. That would be hypocritical. Being a good Christian teacher is not just about how and what we teach. It is equally about who we are. Our lives must reflect our teaching.

Teaching Tip

- Make sure our lives reflect our teaching

Section 7: **Qualities of a Christian Teacher Checklist**

General
- Being enthusiastic
- Being friendly
- Taking an interest in students
- Showing competence
- Having a knowledge of the topic
- Being confident
- Having charisma
- Having a willingness to prepare well
- Showing patience
- Having an ability to listen

Specific
- Being an example to the people
- we teach
- Teaching sound doctrine
- Showing integrity
- Showing appropriate seriousness
- Having sound teaching
- Saying "No" to ungodliness
- Saying "No" to worldly passions
- Living self controlled lives
- Being upright and godly
- Being encouraging
- Not shirking from rebuking
- Not doing anything to make us despised.

Dedication

This book is dedicated to Sir John Rowling who died in January 2020. Knighted for his services to education John was an inspiring classroom teacher then Headmaster loved and respected by his pupils and colleagues. John lived his faith through Christian service in both school, community and church. Education and service was his life. Through his life-long selfless Christian ministry many people came to a belief in Christ. He gave me invaluable advice and encouragement to write this book. Thank you John, my mentor and dear friend.

www.ingramcontent.com/pod-product-compliance
Lightning Source LLC
Chambersburg PA
CBHW071532080526
44588CB00011B/1648